leaf book

Winter Holidays

Hailey's Halloween

Lisa Bullard

illustrated by **Holli Conger**

M **MILLBROOK PRESS · MINNEAPOLIS**

For Caitlin —L.B.

For my little ghost and goblin,
whose funny little tricks are always
a treat! —H.C.

Text and illustrations copyright © 2013 by Lerner Publishing
Group, Inc.

All rights reserved. International copyright secured. No part
of this book may be reproduced, stored in a retrieval system,
or transmitted in any form or by any means—electronic,
mechanical, photocopying, recording, or otherwise—without the
prior written permission of Lerner Publishing Group, Inc., except
for the inclusion of brief quotations in an acknowledged review.

Millbrook Press
A division of Lerner Publishing Group, Inc.
241 First Avenue North
Minneapolis, MN 55401 U.S.A.

Website address: www.lernerbooks.com

Main body text set in Slappy Inline 18/28.
Typeface provided by T26.

Library of Congress Cataloging-in-Publication Data

Bullard, Lisa.
    Hailey's Halloween / by Lisa Bullard ; illustrated by Holli
Conger.
        p.   cm. — (Cloverleaf books—fall and winter holidays)
    Includes index.
    ISBN 978–0–7613–5083–5 (lib. bdg. : alk. paper)
    1. Halloween—Juvenile literature. I. Conger, Holli, ill. II. Title.
GT4965.B85 2013
394.2646—dc23   2011046171

Manufactured in the United States of America
1 – BP – 7/15/12

TABLE OF CONTENTS

Chapter One

My Favorite Holiday

Boo! I'm Hailey. Do you know what tomorrow is? It's October 31.

DECORATIONS

COSTUMES

How to carve your pumpkin

eyeBALLs

That's Halloween. It's my favorite holiday!

SPIDERS
3 FOR $1

I have a **big problem.**

I can't decide what to be for Halloween!

People have worn costumes at Halloween time for many years. Some of the earliest costumes were made from animal skins.

I want the **best costume** ever.
My family is helping me choose.

Chapter Two

Halloween Long Ago

Mom tells me that Halloween started **long ago.**

I know! I'll dress up like a **dinosaur**.
They're from long ago too.

Mom says not that long ago. She's talking about people in Europe called **Celts**. They celebrated something called **Samhain**.

The Celts lived in part of Europe about two thousand years ago. Samhain was at the same time of year that we celebrate Halloween.

The Celts thought **Spirits** visited Earth on Samhain. It sounds scary.

But not as **SCARY** as this **monster** mask, I bet!

Mom says that later, the Christian church made some new holidays.

November 1 became a church holiday about 1,200 years ago. Some people called it All Hallows' Day. The night before—October 31—became All Hallows' Eve. Later, the name changed to Halloween.

The new holidays were at this same time of year.
They were a time to remember people who had died.

So maybe I should dress up as a ghost.

Chapter Three
Halloween Comes to North America

About four hundred years ago, some people moved from Europe to North America. They sailed on big ships. Over time, Halloween became an important day in North America too.

Pirates also sail on big ships. Do you think I should wear a pirate costume?

Halloween has spread to many countries around the world. But the city of Anoka, Minnesota, is known as the Halloween Capital of the World.

I finally found my costume. It's a surprise, though! You can't see it until tomorrow. Right now I have to make my jack-o'-lantern.

Long ago, there weren't pumpkins in Europe. People there carved vegetables such as beets or turnips. They put them out on Halloween to scare away evil spirits. The people who came to North America started carving pumpkins.

I draw a face on my pumpkin. Dad carves it out. Mom puts a light inside.

Look! It's missing more teeth than I am.

Chapter Four

Trick or Treat Day!

At last, it's time to **trick-or-treat!** My friends are waiting. Can you guess what I decided to be?

Many children today go door-to-door on Halloween. They say "trick or treat" at each house. Then people give them candy. People long ago also went door-to-door. They offered to pray for the dead. Then the people in those houses gave them food.

Did you guess right?

People often choose Halloween costumes or decorations that they find scary. This might include bats, spiders, monsters, ghosts, skeletons, or witches. Being scared is a part of Halloween fun!

My **black cat**, Trick, agrees. This really is the **best costume** ever!

Make It Yourself: Face Paint

You can use ingredients from home to make your own easy face paint. Then you can dress up as almost anything you want for Halloween!

Ingredients:
1 teaspoon corn starch
½ teaspoon cold cream
   (a type of face cream)
½ teaspoon water
food coloring

Equipment:
measuring spoons
spoon
medium-size bowl

1) Stir together the corn starch and the cold cream in the bowl.

2) Add water and stir again.

3) Add a drop or two of food coloring to make the color you need.

Try it!
Food coloring usually comes in four colors: red, blue, yellow, and green. Mix red and yellow to make orange. Mix blue and red to make purple. What happens if you mix all four colors together?

GLOSSARY

beets: round, red root vegetables

carve: to cut into a shape

celebrate: to do something special to show that a day is important

Celts (KELTS or SELTS): a group of people who lived in parts of Europe about two thousand years ago

Christian: someone who believes in a religion that follows the life and teachings of Jesus

costume: a special outfit you put on so you look like something else, such as a witch or a ghost

decorations: things that are added to something else to make it look fancy, special, or different

jack-o'-lantern: a pumpkin with a carved-out face and a light inside

Samhain (SAH-win): an old holiday of the Celts

spirits: ghosts

trick-or-treat: to go door-to-door asking for candy

turnips: round, pale-colored root vegetables

BOOKS

Bullard, Lisa. *Trick-or-Treat on Milton Street.* Minneapolis: First Avenue Editions, 2004.
Follow along as Charley discovers that Halloween in his new Milton Street neighborhood is full of surprises.

Heiligman, Deborah. *Celebrate Halloween: With Pumpkins, Costumes, and Candy.*
Washington, DC: National Geographic Society, 2007.
Read more about the history of Halloween and how it is celebrated around the world.

Rustad, Martha E. H. *Fall Pumpkins: Orange and Plump.* Minneapolis: Millbrook Press, 2012.
Learn more about pumpkins, including how they grow and what colors they can be.

Walker, Sally. *Druscilla's Halloween.* Minneapolis: Carolrhoda Books, 2009.
This story about Druscilla the witch reveals why witches ride on broomsticks.

WEBSITES

Enchanted Learning
http://www.enchantedlearning.com/crafts/halloween/
You'll find many Halloween crafts to make at this part of the Enchanted Learning website.

National Geographic Kids
http://kids.nationalgeographic.com/kids/activities/recipes/quick-creepy-recipes/
This part of the National Geographic Kids website has some creepy Halloween recipes. It also has links to pages with costumes you can make and other Halloween activities.

LERNER SOURCE™
Expand learning beyond the printed book. Download free, complementary educational resources for this book from our website, www.lerneresource.com.